Community Helpers

Plumbers

by Tracey Boraas

Consultant:
Robert L. Shepherd
Technical Director, National Association of
Plumbing, Heating, and Cooling Contractors

Bridgestone Books
an imprint of Capstone Press
Mankato, Minnesota

Bridgestone Books are published by Capstone Press
818 North Willow Street, Mankato, Minnesota 56001
http://www.capstone-press.com

Library of Congress Cataloging-in-Publication Data
Boraas, Tracey.
　　Plumbers/by Tracey Boraas.
　　p. cm.—(Community helpers)
　　Includes bibliographical references and index.
　　Summary: An introduction to plumbers, their work, dress, tools, schooling, and
importance in the community.
　　ISBN 0-7368-0073-5
　　1. Plumbers—Vocational guidance—Juvenile literature. 2. Plumbing—Juvenile literature.
[1. Plumbers. 2. Plumbing. 3. Occupations.] I. Title. II. Series: Community helpers (Mankato,
Minn.)
TH6124.B67　1999
696'.1'023—dc21　　　　　　　　　　　　　98-16855
　　　　　　　　　　　　　　　　　　　　　　　　CIP
　　　　　　　　　　　　　　　　　　　　　　　　AC

Editorial Credits
Michael Fallon, editor; James Franklin, cover designer; Sheri Gosewisch, photo researcher

Photo Credits
David F. Clobes, 4
Leslie O'Shaughnessy, 16
Maguire PhotograFX/Joseph P. Maguire, cover, 14
Tom Pantages, 8
Unicorn Stock Photos/Jean Higgins, 10; Dede Gilman, 12; Herbert L. Stormont, 18; Tommy
Dodson, 20
Valan Photos/V. Wilkinson, 6

Table of Contents

Plumbers

Plumbers fix and clean plumbing. Plumbing is the set of water pipes in a building. Some pipes bring in clean water for drinking or bathing. Other pipes carry away waste water. Plumbers help people keep pipes working in homes or other buildings.

What Plumbers Do

Plumbers do many jobs. They fix leaks in pipes. Leaky pipes can waste clean water. Plumbers clear blocked drainpipes. Drainpipes take away dirty water. Plumbers put in fixtures. Some fixtures are toilets, bathtubs, and sinks.

Kinds of Plumbers

There are many kinds of plumbers. Some plumbers work only in homes. Some work only in stores or office buildings. Other plumbers fix city pipes and sewers. Sewers are underground pipes that carry away waste water.

Where Plumbers Work

Plumbers work in many places where there is plumbing. They work in buildings and in homes. They work in small spaces under floors and sinks. Plumbers also work outside. They fix swimming pools and sewers.

Tools Plumbers Use

Plumbers use wrenches to tighten and loosen pipes. They use pipe cutters to make pipes the right sizes. Plumbers also use drain snakes to unblock pipes. Drain snakes are thick wires that fit down pipes.

What Plumbers Wear

Many plumbers wear coveralls. This one-piece suit of clothing fits over other clothes to keep them clean. Some plumbers wear only ordinary clothes. Plumbers also may wear tool belts to hold their tools.

Plumbers and Training

People train for about five years to become plumbers. They learn to be plumbers by working with master plumbers. A master plumber has been a plumber for many years. Master plumbers teach people all the jobs plumbers do.

How People Help Plumbers

People can help plumbers by keeping their plumbing safe. People should only pour liquids such as water down drains. Solid objects could block drainpipes. People also should not block taps with objects. A tap controls the flow of water from a pipe.

How Plumbers Help Others

Plumbers help to keep water safe and clean. People need clean water for drinking and bathing. Plumbers make sure clean water comes in through pipes. They also make sure pipes safely carry away waste water.

Hands on: Learn How Water Pressure Works

Water pressure is a force that pushes water through pipes. Pumps make water pressure in plumbing by pushing water through pipes. Plumbers know how water pressure works. You can learn how water pressure works too.

What You Need

An empty dishwashing soap bottle
Plenty of water
A two-foot rubber hose
Duct tape
A sink or bucket

What You Do

1. Take the cap off the bottle. Fill the bottle with water.
2. Put the cap back on the bottle. Be sure the spout is open.
   Attach the rubber hose to the cap with duct tape.
3. Squeeze the bottle gently over a sink or bucket.
4. Squeeze the bottle hard over a sink or bucket.

What Happens

The hose is like a pipe. By gently squeezing the bottle you make a little water pressure. The water comes out slowly through the hose. You make more water pressure when you squeeze hard. The water rushes out quickly.

Words to Know

master plumber (MASS-tur PLUHM-ur)—a person who has been a plumber for many years

plumbing (PLUHM-ing)—the set of water pipes in a home or building

sewer (SOO-ur)—an underground pipe that carries away waste water

water pressure (WAT-ur PRESH-ur)—a force that pushes water through pipes

wrench (RENCH)—a tool used to tighten or loosen pipes

Read More

Lillegard, Dee, and Wayne Stoker. *I Can Be a Plumber.* Chicago: Children's Press, 1987.

Yardley, Thompson. *Down the Drain: Explore Your Plumbing.* A Lighter Look Book. Brookfield, Conn.: Millbrook Press, 1991.

Internet Sites

Drinking Water Activities for Kids
http://www.epa.gov/OGWDW/kids
Water Questions and Answers: Water Use at Home
http://h2o.usgs.gov/public/watuse/wuqa.home.html

Index